Thresherphobe

Georgia,
best writer at NYU!
Your weird uncle says
you have to keep this forever.

Love,
Mark

PHOENIX POETS

MARK HALLIDAY

Thresherphobe

THE UNIVERSITY OF CHICAGO PRESS
Chicago & London

MARK HALLIDAY is distinguished professor of English at Ohio University. His previous books include *Selfwolf* and *Jab*, both published by the University of Chicago Press. He is also the author of a critical study of Wallace Stevens and many essays on contemporary poets.

The University of Chicago Press, Chicago 60637
The University of Chicago Press, Ltd., London
© 2013 by The University of Chicago
All rights reserved. Published 2013.
Printed in the United States of America

22 21 20 19 18 17 16 15 14 13   1 2 3 4 5

ISBN-13: 978-0-226-03870-4 (paper)
ISBN-13: 978-0-226-03884-1 (e-book)

Library of Congress Cataloging-in-Publication Data
Halliday, Mark, 1949– author.
    Thresherphobe / Mark Halliday.
        pages cm. — (Phoenix poets)
    Poems.
    ISBN 978-0-226-03870-4 (paperback : alkaline paper)
    ISBN 978-0-226-03884-1 (e-book)
    I. Title. II. Series: Phoenix poets.
    PS3558.A386T47 2013
    811'.54—dc23   2012033559

♾ This paper meets the requirements of ANSI/NISO Z39.48-1992 (Permanence of Paper).

Du schnell vergehendes Daguerreotyp
in meinen langsamer vergehenden Händen.

Rainer Maria Rilke

That my chaff might fly; my grain lie, sheer and clear.

Gerard Manley Hopkins

Still,
we mourn what we mourn.
Even if, when it sank to its irreplaceable knees,
when its unique throat closed behind a sigh,
no dust rose to redden a whole year's sunsets,
no one unwittingly busy
two thousand miles away jumped at the sound,
no ashes rained on ships in the merciless sea.

Sarah Lindsay

We do what we can.

Paul Mariani

Put on your pretty red dress
Let's go see about this mess

Hank Ballard & the Midnighters

CONTENTS

ACKNOWLEDGMENTS

Some of the poems in this book first appeared in journals or magazines as follows:

The Chattahoochee Review: "Ted's Elegiac Work"
Ecotone: "Quite Frankly"
Fifth Wednesday: "Ducks Not in Row" and "Ferguson High"
Green Mountains Review: "Flang Flight"
The Hopkins Review: "Thanks for Your Book"
Hunger Mountain: "Reader Depressed"
Indiana Review: "Lingo Bistro"
The Iowa Review: "240 Sneakers"
The Kenyon Review: "There We Were"
Little Star: "La Marquise de Gloire," "Double Reverse," and
    "Just In Time"
Los Angeles Review: "Sweet and Dandy"
Passages North: "New New Poetics"
Poemeleon (online): "His Alley Metaphor" and "Pathos of the
    Momentary Smile"
Poetry Review (London): "Livin' in the World"
Slate (online): "Frankfort Laundromat"
Upstreet: "Lois in the Sunny Tree"

"Lois in the Sunny Tree" also appeared in *Joining Music With Reason*, edited by Christopher Ricks (Oxfordshire, UK: Waywiser Press, 2010).

"Frankfort Laundromat" also appeared in *Poets of the New Century*, edited by Roger Weingarten and Richard M. Higgerson (Boston: David R. Godine Press, 2001).

"Unconversation" appeared in *The Breath of Parted Lips: Poems from the Robert Frost Place* (Fort Lee, NJ: CavanKerry Press, 2001).

LOIS IN THE SUNNY TREE

When in August 1920 I smiled for the camera
from my perch on the limb of a sun-spangled tree,
says Lois, long dead now but humorously seven years old then,
with a giant ribbon in my hair, the sorrow of living in time
was only very tiny and remote in some far corner of my mind

and for me to know then, as I smiled for that camera
in Michigan in the summer of 1920
that you would peer thoughtfully and admiringly
into my happy photographed eyes eighty-some years later
would have been good for me only in a very tiny and remote way.

QUITE FRANKLY

They got old, they got old and died. But first—
okay but first they composed plangent depictions
of how much they lost and how much cared about losing.
Meantime their hair got thin and more thin
as their shoulders went slumpy. Okay but

not before the photo albums got arranged by them,
arranged with a niftiness, not just two or three
but eighteen photo albums, yes eighteen eventually,
eighteen albums proving the beauty of them (and not someone else),
them and their relations and friends, incontrovertible

playing croquet in that Bloomington yard,
floating on those comic inflatables at Dow Lake,
giggling at the Dairy Queen, waltzing at the wedding,
building a Lego palace on the porch,
holding the baby beside the rental truck,
leaning on the Hemingway statue at Pamplona,
discussing the eternity of art in that Sardinian restaurant.

Yes! And so, quite frankly—at the end of the day—
they got old and died okay sure but quite frankly
how much does that matter in view of
the eighteen photo albums, big ones
thirteen inches by twelve inches each
full of such undeniable beauty?

SWEET AND DANDY

Music poured from the big brown house

It was sweet and dandy, sweet and dandy
and a man sixty years old may have passed
along the dark sidewalk wearing a sensible raincoat
and a spelling-out of his thought would be

Bright oblivious mediocrity of common animal-vigorous youth
as he moved further into the chilly dark outside

but wait just a second, sir,
be careful of glibness, because I was there
amidst the reggae, I the me in 1973
as we tried to embrace the hour
(because if we didn't do it, who would?)
having already heard a rumor that I would become you
so I danced hilarious with Maggie P. and Mary K.

RETURN TO ELMGROVE

In this dream I fly above a thousand thousand suburban trees
as the crow flies unconstrained by streets of time
I do fly swoon-swooping weightlessly
to my house of thirty-eight years ago
where I should leave notes for my old friends
but where is a pencil there must be a pencil in the kitchen
down that hall of shadow light of ghosted air
I float into the kitchen a bowl of cereal appears in my hand
my lover of thirty-eight years ago appears beside me
and leans her head on my shoulder weightlessly
I should give her a note
to remind her that we must have so much to remember
so much to hang on to
there must be a blank page in that book near her hand
I should give her a note explaining how things have gone
but she seems so quietly nostalgic there is nothing to do
everything is over I have no pencil only this
bowl of cereal which is so much heavier than it looks.

VACATION DAY IN 1983

Sunny day in Chatham and we've said we'll play tennis
but we're all doing things. Annie is working on her bibliography.
Carl needs to record in his notebook a long dream he had last night.
At one point in the dream he said to these two Korean girls
"I'm being chased by a crazy lady with a machine gun,
if you can help me in any way I'll be very grateful."
Carl in his dream is polite and respectful
as if to keep chaos under superficial control.
He disappears into a bedroom of the cottage.
I add sugar to the coffee I should have drunk an hour ago.
Peter notices the picture on the Morton Salt box
and says when he was a kid he wore one of those slick yellow raincoats
and Annie says he must have been so cute. Peter says
oh you'd say that about any kid in a yellow raincoat.
Peter puts *Nashville Skyline* on the stereo. I'm trying to read
D. H. Lawrence on what a novel should and shouldn't be.
Peter says "Girl From the North Country" might be
Dylan's only song about his early life but I say there must be others,
Peter thinks of "Something There Is about You" on *Planet Waves*
and I think of that one about riding on a train going west
though I forget the title. Carl reappears and lies down on the sofa
with *The Soft Machine* by Burroughs. We're all like plants trying
to locate the right kind of sunlight to grow in. I write this insight
carefully on an envelope. Peter says "Tennis agenda?"
and Annie says "Just two more citations
and I'm ready to go." Peter finds his white socks. I'm nursing
my precious tepid coffee. Everybody senses that I'll be the reason
we don't get out the door soon. One side of *Nashville Skyline* is already over

and Peter puts on an album by Kraftwerk. I roll my eyes
and Peter grins at my ignorance of what is Euro-cool.
He and Annie eat a few strawberries. Lawrence wants *life*.
Carl sees a rabbit outside and shouts in his Star Trek voice
"Captain, the Xyrilians have us surrounded!"
I look for the can of tennis balls, someone already found it,
suddenly everyone is outside at the car
except me—life just happens absurdly full absurdly quick
ripeness is you know what all right Peter stop honking
away we go.

THERE WE WERE

You know what's so dumb about your abject devotion to the past?
I mean this fetishy nursing of the traces of everything you ever did,
like the photo of Laurinda wearing her buckskin fringe
at that party in the field behind the Kingfisher Pub
where you thought she was hinting you up to be her Sundance Kid
or like those letters Margie Lou sent you on lavender paper
ostensibly about John Le Carré but really about possible romance
in Pittsburgh. What's so dumb is—oh my god—you *so* don't get it—

when you cherish those two-dimensional traces of whatever was
you are basically focusing your *existence* on something that does not *exist*.
Because the past is nothing but shadows spilled over other shadows
in your head
                 and by the way that book you published seven years ago?
That book is ancient. That book is practically as dead as Thomas Hardy.
It's so funny how you can't admit this. That book,
okay I know you think you poured your best self into it
but even if that were true it would still be a *gone* self that got poured,
a now hypothetical person who merely resembles from certain angles
the person we see in those photos from a decade ago that you keep
flipping through or slipping into your wallet, that person is essentially dead

but I know you think when you stare at an old picture or old letter
there's a certain way to sigh
that breathes magic life back into the ancient traces
and it's like you're the shaman of this cult, this wacky superstitious cult of
Ah there I was, there we were

so I have to hear about when you and Rosanna sang "Waterfall"
at some club in Toronto or when you and Nancy sang "Tossin' and Turnin'"
at that summer camp oh my god how pathetically quaint!
So my suggestion to you is: Wake up and *live*. Like, *today*.
And if you decide to do that, call me because frankly
I think we need to talk about last night.

HISTORIC SHIRT

Ran into Alyssa and Todd and Alyssa said "I like your shirt"
and I laughed because it's obviously very old and she said
"But it looks so soft and comfortable" and I agreed
and Alyssa said "And that little heart is so sweet"
referring to the red velvet heart sewn on the left shoulder
so I said "There's a lot of history in that" and then had to explain
that my first wife sewed the heart on this shirt
for her boyfriend before me—and Alyssa said
"Wow, that seems symbolic of something!" and Todd laughed
and I said "It probably means that I refuse to let go of
any trace of the past" and Alyssa said "Or maybe it means
you refuse to be oppressed by the past" and I said
"That sounds good" and Todd sort of half smiled and Alyssa said
"You accept the past so it can't then turn around and bite you"
and for a half second this idea sparkled alarmingly in the air
and then we all smiled in order to let the scene end

and Alyssa walked away arm in arm with her new husband
to go on making the life that would be their past together.

THANKS TO ACKER BILK

There is a mosaic. It makes the background
on which amidst which can appear the figures
upon which in which you have concentrated
desire, fear, fascination, worry, love, regret.
There is for you this mosaic
assembled in bits every day this mosaic in which—
through which—by which and maybe even for which
you have gone on living; there had to be this context;

for example in 1962 there was that melody
"Stranger on the Shore"—
played on clarinet by a man named Acker Bilk—

I didn't care, it was just some tune that older people probably liked
and it just showed up on the radio—in the kitchen or from car windows
a dozen times—a hundred times?—in the years—I didn't care—
it wasn't rock and roll!
                              Yet it formed
one bit in the mosaic—
                              forgotten and then
decades later revealing itself to be unforgettable:
the melody of
one version of
eternal wistfulness in which
you must slowly staringly wander until you die.

For the chance to build a mosaic I am grateful
to my parents and America and chaotic Earth
and I send now this belated Thank You to Acker Bilk.

FRANKFORT LAUNDROMAT

Smooth plastic chair, thoughtless heavy air, my eyes closed,
my father walked in, he had his bag of laundry.
My laundry was in a machine already, some forty years prior to my death.
Like me my father was alive, he was eighty-one. We were both
sunburned and tired, this was after hours on the beach,
after the picnic, after when the Honda got stuck in sand,
this was after, then came the laundry; my father said
"Did you get burned much?" I said "Not too bad" and
he put his clothes in a machine. Small box of Tide.
My eyes closed over *The Burden of the Past* by W. J. Bate
and my eyes opened, hot room smell of soap and hot fabric,
and my father's shirt was dark pink, like a heart I half thought
but my eyes closed, after the hours in the sun and
buying the stuff for sandwiches for everybody and
making sure Nick and the girls didn't really hurt the seagulls
and after Asa felt sick at lunch and we took him to his mother
and after the humid tennis and so my eyes closed. . . .
Then they opened
                    apparently for more living,

I put my laundry in a dryer and my father was reading the *New Republic*,
he was concentrating, with his reading glasses on, and caring
about the truth, despite all the sun and all the sandwiches and tennis and
      driving
and I loved him reading there in his dark pink shirt. But my head was
gravitational to the floor, my chin to my neck, I tried to read
The Burden of the Past and closed my eyes some forty years before my death
unless it comes sooner, and a fly shifted from *People* magazine on a table
to my father's shoulder to a Certs wrapper on the floor

and the fly was the word *and*. . . .
                                    Then my clothes were dry
and impressively hot and I held my face to a hot dry towel—

I wanted to live—to live enough—to be *living*—but to live all day
with the sunburn and the smell of Tide and the gravitation—was it possible?
But my father was still reading. He still cared about the *New Republic*—
therefore with the normal courage of any son or any daughter
I folded my laundry and carried it out to the Honda for more living,
as my father went on reading for truth in his shirt dark pink like a heart.

240 SNEAKERS

This old guy sits in a car beside a road in Illinois
near a five-way intersection at the edge of a town;
there's a Dairy Queen a hundred yards away
but it probably hasn't opened yet.
The old man is a little confused about whether he is heading
south or east but everything will eventually be clear.

If his daughter were here she would be impatient
but she is in Montgomery, Alabama, at her job
and that is a clear fact.
He sits in the car and looks down at his shoes—sneakers
because he knows he's still a boy really
though people don't see it; a boy trying to sneak quietly
through the world without getting caught by
whatever catches people. . . .

                                        How many pairs of sneakers
has he owned—he estimates one hundred and twenty pairs—
how many of those two hundred and forty sneakers still exist?
The oldest ones must be decayed, softened, obliterated
in some landfill in Indiana—Indiana landfill—
Indiana landfill

                        —a few birds twitter
in trees near his car—there was a rainstorm earlier
and now the birds have to start their day again;
there's a question he needs to ask—
he watches the Dairy Queen carefully:
he can walk softly to the ice cream window when it opens

and if the person there seems impatient
he can order one scoop, they might have peach ice cream,
then he can ask about directions—sometimes the first answer
isn't the one you need so you have to ask again—
rushing just gets you to the wrong spot too soon;
so the plan is to ask, and wait for an answer that makes some sense.

TED'S ELEGIAC WORK

Ted's father died, and in the next eighteen months
Ted needed to write about his father and death

and if you look at these writings sympathetically
you see that they are intelligent and sensitive, in some respects,
they make many delicate choices among words.

But if you step back, several steps back,
you see that basically what Ted says about his father's death
is what you mostly could have predicted,
including gratitude for the dad's patience
when the boy had trouble learning some outdoorsy physical skill
and regret for silences near the end
when they could have discussed the family's way of life, or Shakespeare,

but the Angel of Meaningfulness is not distracted or dismayed
by such broad parameters of predictability,
the A. of M. is interested in the most subtle shades of embodied spirit

and the A. of M. says quietly "Good for you, Ted,
your writing is worthy and in a related way so are you,
and I like the way you walk as if amused by distance
and the way you look at winter trees
with a sense of their metaphorical dignity
and the way you speak humorously to children."

Unfortunately the A. of M. is so soft-spoken
Ted is never totally sure he hears the heavenly voice
except when it ventriloquizes through a human reader who says
"I love you" or
"I enjoyed the stuff about your dad, especially
the detail about the sardines with mustard."

BEV AND BROADWAY

And what if Bev had lived, could have lived
to love one more Broadway musical, learning
all the words to the six best songs and quoting them
It takes a lot of love to make a pound
hilariously out of context while shopping or cooking

that would only be quantity, do you see—
that would only be a kind of repetition,
essentially redundant—after ten or twelve Broadway shows
one more for her to love and be funny about
would be only a change of quantity, do you see,
only addition—
               one more, one less, this is as nothing

in the marble-columned perspective of eternity
from the mountaintop where human lives are calmly nodded to
—whether strangely long and generously allowed like mine
or cut short like Bev's—
nodded to calmly, do you see

which is why I don't get along with eternity
Love is a very light thing
though it be indispensable because there she can seem to rest.

SPUNKTILIO AWAITS THE BIOGRAPHER

Where is the biographer? The biographer is delayed.

I have been ready for the biographer since I turned sixty-three
as a ripeness had arrived by then, a kind of fullness of richness of
ramifications of everything I had ever written or said.
Ripeness continued then in its red-orange-blue radiance
for some years—some several—until

a slight fading became detectable—and then unignorable—
when I was sixty-eight—one day my meditations written neatly
(not scribbled) in the margins of books from thirty years ago
emitted a mild dull cloudy odor of I'm-just-little-old-me

and now I am strangely seventy-two
with my cabinets full of notebooks and files still ready
but coated with unwanted thin layers of humility
and the biographer not only has not arrived,
he or she has seemed not to care to exist. He or she can't be bothered

and now my fear (beyond the old fear of being overlooked and defeated)
is that if the biographer were to show up now—briskly optimistic,
in his or her early forties, with brilliantly tiny recorders and cameras
and questions that confuse the pale blue of Connecticut in 1976
with the humid gray of Philadelphia in 1985
and quick dry hands reducing my cabinets to paragraphs—

I won't care enough
to fight for what by now has come to seem
a truth with too many disorderly and unmajestic attachments.
How softly away hath my ripeness flown.
Alack, Spunktilio! Thou shalt not be known.

VISIONARY AGE 79

I remember stuff extremely long ago
which is all quietly beautiful-sad because
it is really long ago and it wears the lace
of the enigma of memory—let me say that
again: it wears the enigma, or rather
the lace of the enigma of memory

to which I respond soft-pulsingly
with an unchanged astonishment that has
no name (except "unchanged astonishment")
which means of course nobody can steal it—
it's mine like a purple marble I had
in my pocket seventy years ago

as I roamed the mustard hills
among cows and sheep and dreams and horseplop
and this unchanged astonishment
has been my bread and butter
for fifty years so I will
keep riding this old soft nag

till the final stable out there
beyond those clouds of sheep
and those dreams of cows
including some strangely blue cows
which smell strangely like cold stone
yet also like excellent bread and butter

YVETTE VICKERS

Suppose you hold in one hand the July 1959 *Playboy*
in which the Playmate was Yvette Vickers
born Yvette Vedder in Kansas City in 1928

and in the other hand the *New York Times* of May 5, 2011,
with an article entitled "Mummified Body Found
in Former Actress's Home"—

in one hand the lavish female human physicality
that must have signified to my father
either sublimity or one hell of a good substitute for sublimity

(Yvette trying to remain herself while cooperating
with the cameramen and photo-shoot director,
Yvette caught in some mix of contempt and pride)

in the other hand the article telling how a Ms. Savage
noticed spiderwebs over the door of the dilapidated
house in Beverly Hills—"The heat and the lights were still on. . . .

I didn't even realize it was a body. It was so compressed,
to maybe a third as thick as a human body should be"—
holding at once these two pieces of the story of Yvette

what do you have? Insight? Something fresh to say?
What you have is evidence that *Time is a creep*—
but you knew that.

AFTER YOU DIE

When you die it's going to be a very big deal.
It won't be something that people just take in stride.
When the news hits there will be the moment of wide-eyed shock—
then everyone will know the world has changed.

And "everyone" doesn't mean simply your family
plus a scatter of relatives and close friends (eight or nine friends,
thirteen or fourteen friends)—not by a long shot—
"everyone" in this case refers to a constituency so extensive
and so resistant to limited definition as to be in a way

infinite: the people who *knew*—who carried in their souls
the glow of knowledge of how you were so much more
than just "a good enough person." . . . They will feel an ache
as they stand still holding the phone and staring out a window
at Nature—enduring, or budding, oblivious—
and Nature's oblivion will be what they refuse to imitate.

In the next few days of course there will be the flurry
of emails and postings—people saying "terrible news"
and "such a loss"—but then when this would normally taper off
there will instead be an expansion, rippling outward,
as more and more people feel the world's new absence;
they will trade anecdotes about how _____ you were,
how _____ and yet at the same time how _____.
People you only met once or twice will say
the world has lost a certain combination of powers
never to be seen again. The way you verbed,

the way you verbed and then promptly verbed,
the priceless way you had the nerve to verb
when others were fearful or shy. . . .

"It's as if a world has ended"—this will be said
not by just one mourner but at least five. . . .
Your family of course will hold a tearful memorial service
with sixty people present—no, eighty-five people—but soon
it will be obvious
that at least two hundred more people feel an intense need
for a collective ceremonial honoring of you—
actually almost four hundred people—and so

there will be a great evening in an auditorium—packed!—
people standing in the aisles—everyone unwilling to let
the phenomenon of you slip off into the vagueness of sad news
from last month, last season, last year;
and the speakers will include not only your closest friends
from the Nineties and the Eighties and the Seventies
causing the crowd to laugh weepingly with tales of
how you _____ in the middle of the Museum of Modern Art
and how you could _____ with your eyes closed
and how you once got an entire audience to sing "Lonesome Traveler"
in a reggae rhythm—
                        not only your friends evoking
but also five individuals you might have considered enemies
including the man who notoriously described your work as
"frothy, undisciplined and ultimately useless"—
he will lean into the microphone and confess
that when he wrote that critique he was sick
with jealousy of you, of how you combined
talent with honor. When the crowd applauds him
they will really be applauding you.

Then two weeks, even three may pass
until it becomes clear that so many more people need
a formal and public way to commemorate you!
An event in New York will be organized
and virtually all the smart people in New York will want to be there.
Some of the twenty-seven speakers at the New York event
will be individuals who never knew you on a personal level
but who long to express their appreciation for your work:
each according to his or her predilections will try to identify
its key qualities—*verve* and *buoyancy* and *sparkle*
will be words frequently used, but also
sympathy, *generosity*, and *candor*.
Someone will read aloud your intense yet witty letter to *Harper's*
about the moral necessity of something something
(and a few listeners will remember this longer than anything else).
Tears will well up more than once—more than three times—
not least when an old friend tells—with three or actually five
vivid examples, how in social situations—
parties, receptions, dinners, classes—you always sought out
the shyest, loneliest person and by gentle friendliness helped
her or him feel part of the evening's success.

And when three of your former lovers go to the podium
and, almost unrehearsed, sing in harmony "If Not for You"
(claiming that you once laughingly requested this)
the effect will be fabulous
and it will seem right and inevitable that
three of your former lovers can sing like angels!

What an evening! What an event!

And then—a month after that in another city
there will have to be a third big memorial gathering,
and some persons who will have attended all three will claim
that this event was the most moving of all.

And even after that
a number—quite a number—of your friends and admirers
will still—gazing into silver dawn light through white curtains—
still long to testify to your significance,
still feel unsatisfied

but you won't feel that way; you won't think
any more recognition is required.

CLASSIC BLUNDER

After a noticeably happy day I sleep—
and wake at dawn to a sudden sense of having erred.
What have I done? I've made the classic blunder:
the blunder of living onward forwardly
toward some disappointing future—
what a fool—I should have lived

not forwardly but sideways or circularly
to stay in days like (what now has to be called) yesterday.
Instead I've allowed the sun
already to start pouring through the curtains
the diminishments and inferiorities
of a crude and unsentimental next day.
To keep that train from leaving the station
must call for some incredible level of concentration.

JUST IN TIME

We will cook again that happy eggplant dish before the end
We're going to learn "Lay Down Your Weary Tune" before the end

All the jams in the refrigerator will be appreciated
All the photos in the album will be approximately dated

Not long before the long quiet you'll have one more thing to say
A lover in blue jeans from far back is walking slowly this way

threading the crowd with seriously poised maneuver
to reach you just before everything is over.

FERGUSON HIGH

Those boys who go to Ferguson High—they must know things
I don't have a chance to know. Their lives have hard edges.
The intersections on both sides of Ferguson High are complicated
with different rules for different times of day, and a cop,
and they have numbered stickers for parking
and their football uniform is purple and black—that's amazing.
Ours is just red and white. My life is so obvious.
My life is like, Monday Tuesday Wednesday.
It's like "Yeah, of course"
and there's nothing in it that somebody would call experience
if the somebody was Vanessa Prout or Michelle Boudreaux.
The car my parents let me drive is just a blob on wheels,
silver gray like some old lady's hair, it smells like a dog
even though we don't have a dog
and the back seat is full of my dad's old golf bag.
Imagine going to pick up Vanessa Prout with this car.
Or Michelle Boudreaux. It can't be imagined.
So it makes sense if they both go out with guys from Ferguson
according to what I heard today in study hall. Because

Michelle and Vanessa naturally want *experience*
which is what I for some reason can never have
because wherever I am life just automatically becomes
exactly what you would have expected while you were dozing off
in study hall. I don't see why I deserve this—
did I *choose* to be a decent dweeb
who has to drive a silver-gray bag of dreams past Ferguson High

to the mall to get a replacement lint-filter screen
for the dryer in the basement of my totally obvious house?
I don't remember choosing that.

Ferguson High—their uniforms are purple and black like a mean secret.
And somewhere there's a girl shaped like Michelle only taller
with swirly black hair and a purple flower between her teeth oh hell
oh *hell* oh hell.

SORORITY SOFTBALL

Those girls gathered at home plate, their arms around each other's shoulders:
they must be a sorority softball team. On such a hot day
they've had a long dusty practice and now their coach must be
offering last bits of wisdom. Girls—young women.
Their calves—the sweaty glisten of their calves in the low but still fierce
sunshine—maybe fourteen young women—girls—two calves per—
that's twenty-eight strong tanned calves over there at home plate.
Let no critic be paid for explaining that my focus
on the twenty-eight glistening calves is dehumanizing!
I have my own struggle to keep some human dignity
over here old enough to be their (young!) grandfather
driving past beyond the left-field fence.
To say that their team's reality, their version of humanity
excludes mine
feels like a crazily calm understatement on this still-hot day.

DOUBLE REVERSE

In touch football my favorite idea was always the double reverse.
At least once in every set of downs I proposed it in the huddle.
Normally my teammates just said "No way"
and called a simple short pass play

but once in a while, if we were far ahead—
or more likely, far behind with darkness falling,
they'd grin—"Why not?"

It's the improbability that's sublime:
handoff to the halfback running left, then
he hands off to the left end running right who then—
fabulously, dreamingly—hands off to the right end
running left!

        Also, the dramatization of the idea
that progress is not the only measure of beauty and
so much can be done without (for a while) *getting* anywhere.

The defense is meant to be utterly baffled, frantic,
desperately ambivalent, unable to fathom the weird
emergence of fresh possibilities—
although in reality—
        in actual reality the play ended
either with a collision or fumble amid the three handoffs
or a deluge of undeluded omniscient cynical tacklers—

because in real life we seemed to take so long
to reach the gorgeous third handoff—hours passed
as we dream-sprinted behind that line of scrimmage. . . .

Still I would call that play again
in any huddle if any team would listen.
I've been a loser on countless muddy fields
and loved not the defeats but the *amazing chance*—

huddle up now, huddle up, I've got an idea.

WIDE RECEIVER

In the huddle you said "Go long—get open"
and at the snap I took off along the right sideline
and then cut across left in a long arc
and I'm sure I was open at several points—
glancing back I saw you pump-fake more than once
but you must not have been satisfied with what you saw downfield
and then I got bumped off course and my hands touched the turf
but I regained my balance and dashed back to the right
I think or maybe first left and then right
and I definitely got open but the throw never came—

maybe you thought I couldn't hang on to a ball flung so far
or maybe you actually can't throw so far
but in any case I feel quite open now,
the defenders don't seem too interested in me
I sense only open air all around me
though the air is getting darker and it would appear
by now we're well into the fourth quarter
and I strongly doubt we can afford to settle for
dinky little first downs if the score is what I think it is

so come on, star boy, fling a Hail Mary
with a dream-coached combination of muscle and faith
and I will gauge the arc and I will not be stupidly frantic
and I will time my jump and—I'm just going to say
in the cool gloaming of this weirdly long game
it is not impossible that I will make the catch.

LA MARQUISE DE GLOIRE

Though it's all too clear how unimpressed you are by a *cri de coeur*
and wafting away unhugged is from your perspective *de rigueur*
of schemes to rendezvous with you I'm still a restless *entrepreneur*

The thought of you converts my favorite main dishes into *hors d'oeuvres*

My addiction to the tingling you induce is a *fait accompli*

Each drifting day is another page in the secret book whose *dénouement*
never arrives, while your fleeting glances lock me into this
                   unfinishable *roman à clef*

The idea that any one remembered moment at a party or picnic was
my sole forever lost chance to touch you must be a *cul de sac*

When my projects for a prudent career try to stand up
your voice remembered administers the *coup de grâce*
and my *mélange* of bright ideas becomes a mere *potpourri*

How I would love to believe this dance is a *folie à deux*

The way you stride across Memorial Drive is a *tour de force*
but glimpses across traffic make a paper-thin *raison d'être*

Your recent exit is implicit in many a *mise en scène*

It's as if you heard me approaching for a *tête à tête*
and you slipped into the elevator with your tall boots and *sangfroid*

Always you get to *reculer* and I never seem to *mieux sauter*—

Still I will keep an eye out for you on every *rez-de-chaussée.*

FLANG FLIGHT

The voice to escape is that of the reasonable neighbor
who thinks the gas company should be called about seepage
or the decent colleague holding a memo or small plastic cup
of atrocious sherry. Let our heads not live in a committee. . . .
Mention a tree now. Why a tree
don't ask just do it quickly. There is a tall—a silver
maple, a tall silver maple stands into the pale silver afternoon
—say silver again—let us call afternoon "dobrama"—
the tall the stately tall the noble silver maple stands
into the pale dobrama. Fine. Noble? Why noble
noble because not speaking

oh. But—we can't go there. Then where. Must flee—

Ordonio and Tagliata!
                    Cut to their lips
fitting in a pink mutuality way way beyond the physical (but
still warm wet warm wet still). How lightly whished
are the tresses of Tagliata as from the castle urgedly
they dash! Jinking and prinking of the bells on their saddles . . .
Do the hooves of their steeds touch the mire?
Oh of course you don't scare us with that question
not now when we know where T. and O. will go!
Mire, call it mud, no problem, plashing up upon
the skirts of Tagliata silky whishy and upon
the brookling gandried buckskin trunched spats of tall
Ordonio. Those garments can be washed and
better still—can be taken off—

Tagliata—and Ordonio:
they ride, there they ride 'mongst silver oaks
a-galloping through the cooling misty dobrama.
Is the inn forthwith ahead? Oh it is, the inn does wait
ahead in a green shadowed flang of the forest
with casks of sun-tickled hint-swirled vintage
and is there a bed? There is,
a bed is absolutely there with pillows downy smooth like Dairy Queen
and so!—Ah,
so ah. And we shall have escaped; have escaped—unless
don't say unless
well but unless they find that issues arise, issues of

communication cooperation and commonality among
people matching skills and tools
for people for congruence of long-term goals and trust
to sustain growth of mutually beneficial—
damn—

        we are back at the decent meeting.

DUCKS NOT IN ROW

I thought our understanding was that you would meet me
at a certain Brazilian beach resort. Gina? Jennifer? Michelle?
Did we somehow not get our ducks in a row? Were we not quite
on the same page as regards the certain Brazilian beach resort?
There we were to sip tall yellow drinks in the softening air;
the breeze would be almost comically gentle;
we would stroll on the white sand watching a lithe sloop
as it crosses the bay with slim buoyant confidence
and then we'd be back on the terrace with further drinks—
I love the word *terrace* and it goes splendidly with *drinks*—

and soon our sex would be so all-encompassing
and so easy and wet and unambivalent
the world would become a sphere of sheer affirmation.
The sheets would be green and yellow. Your freckles
would resemble those of Sharon who played cowboys with me
in 1957. As I recall, this was the gist of our understanding.
Jennifer? Or Gina? Michelle, is your message device even charged?
Somewhere along the line a ball was dropped, because
we definitely have not met at a certain Brazilian beach resort!
We are not on the access road to such, and in fact
around the word *Brazil* there is starting to form a penumbra
of what some adult might call mild-old-joke-tinged-with-pathos.

PATHOS OF THE MOMENTARY SMILE

Like nearly all women under sixty she would have deftly
avoided meeting the eyes of an unknown man—

but occasionally an exception happens by chance
and her unconscious skill at avoidance gets instantly
replaced by a human generosity which is either
inherently feminine or gender-trained, as you please;

she glanced at me exactly when I glanced at her
in the store at the mall and so she gave me
that momentary slight smile which implies

*Though many men are dangerous, and I do not intend
to suggest the slightest likelihood that you and I will
meet or talk, much less make love and
much less together conceive a sweet helpless child,
still our eyes have just met and in this there is
an undeniable contact between your humanity and mine
and you are probably coping with some difficulties
of masculine humanity while I cope with those
of feminine humanity; and so I wish you well.*

Her smile said this
but I did not smile back because—
because guys don't do that—because
we are strong and separate and firm and without softness!

So then the next moment had come and we had walked apart
in our two differently inflected kinds of routine loneliness.

HUGE PARTY

We did go to the huge party—we arrived at the open door—music
poured out into the driveway, I said it was Dixieland but you said zydeco
and we could not pause to decide—the door was open
and we had been casually invited or we seemed to have been included
in some sweeping insouciantly generous invitation—we stepped

through the door, the music sprayed itself over us like a perfume,
we wove a path between ravenously witty talkers to the next room
and the next—it was a huge party and we kept saying so—
any amount of stuff was happening in full swing in seven rooms

and later it was over

but we did arrive at the huge party—we did step in I remember
how we passed through that casually open door and wove
a path like a canoe in turbulent waters through the brilliant talkers
who could have been speaking Danish or Korean or Farsi
and we smiled as if to say "No problem, we're here, we're with it
we're part of it part of the whole thing the huge—"

and we ate those fabulous stuffed grape leaves
and that server Marisa with the sly side-glances and severe eyebrows
gave us highballs which we drank fast so as not to be sheepish
and Adele with her endless silk scarves touched our elbows
and led us out to the balcony to meet the famous Dr. Smooshchenia
though we failed to catch why he was famous—he said "Rotterdam"
and "acculturation" and "neo-expressionist" and "*fin-de-siècle*" and "false sublime"
and "defamiliarization" and "Svengali" and "*Dasein*" and "enigma"
and "arpeggio" and "paradigm shift" and Marisa came near with stuffed olives

and Dr. Smoosh was gone—carried away on a yacht made of Adele's scarves—
we watched some dancers dance, they never looked at us—
a huge party we said—we met two Sylvias and everyone else knew which
Sylvia was the one who made the terrifying movie but we never got it straight
and the nephew of the hostess made his helicopter land on a pie—it was
a coconut cream pie—but who was the hostess after all? Not Adele?
François seemed to be explaining but his accent was so thick—
then in a hallway Sherrie's aunt said something about Orville in Burma
or was it Irma from Louisville—Sherrie was the companion of either
François or the man with the Chilean flag on his tie—the music

suddenly was so loud we squeezed through a door and into another room
where Michael and Madelyn made dry remarks about Dr. Smoosh
as if we were friends—I turned to find another drink—

and then it was over and we were home—
the party had occurred in the past
and we sat on the back porch holding our heads in our hands
as the morning spread blank and untransformed;
the fat motorcycle man next door was cursing the Sanitation Department
and the Greek lady's Doberman trotted in chained circles
endlessly tense endlessly craving for something to *happen*—

we leaned back in our creaking chairs
waiting for the rain of specks of the huge party to stop falling
and a quiet that would dispose of questions

Did we really go to the party?
Where is the huge party now?

UNCONVERSATION

Among people
you sort of half step toward me but then a faltering prevails
due to tiny transparent bats that bounce off our cheekbones:
they are the conversations that probably won't happen.
I look down. I look into my tepid coffee.
You glance at my ear;
I glance at your eyebrow;
you pass through space
between wool shoulders and we are relieved
and we are sad. Pelted by tiny glass bats
we wobble sideways around the noisy room.
This room is so full of people, folks, persons, people,
les hommes et les femmes—
les hommes et les femmes, les hommes et les femmes les hommes et les femmes—
aieeee!
At moments I seem to love the way they stand and the way they tilt their heads.
However, they are manifestly *too much.*
The male gaze, the female gaze, the person-as-such gaze,
I want a helmet with a visor!

I look at a light on a building across the street
and I'm grateful for the distance between me and this light.
The light is small and cold and far and so
it is safe and safe is good, safe is a type of beauty,
it is the Convenient Transcendent.
You are down the hall. I think I hear your voice
saying something something father or farther,

something something mixing them or Michigan,
something something Thomas Edison or Tommy's medicine.
Your voice is a rag of a flag waving from a schooner near the horizon,
it is a flaring of the string section in the symphony of
what has occurred elsewhere, for other people,
in the green field of the conversations that do happen.
I accept this

with a kind of dry creaking of the skin on my face
which seems to me the symptom of my courage
in coping with humanity fatigue. People
are often attractive but *always* tiring
so it's no wonder the room is filling up
with the conversations that will not have happened.
Serious questions and serious answers never uttered
are flicking against the furniture, flying caterpillars
that will never become life-affirming Lepidoptera.

—Wait, didn't I say they were glass bats?
But what's the difference if no one is listening?
And I have had enough of metaphor now.
Metaphor is sticky and gummy like—like humanness.
This gray crust tufting my eyebrows and casting a shadow
across the dry creaking of my face—
it is the detritus from the smashing of tiny creatures
made of untalked talk! It is humanity
that has tufted me with gray crust.

. . . And so I look down.
I look to my far cold light.
Good night.

Tomorrow, though—
I might wake up provisionally uncrusted
and we could run into each other
in some bookstore or café
in Greenfield, Terre Haute, or Santa Fe
and there you, you with your tantalizing alterity
and your charismatic clean hair
and your insouciant apparent infinity
may once again impinge.

BEFORE DAWN

Before dawn I disappointed my great mentor
by stupidly inviting a dull moralistic frowzy colleague
to the lunch at which my mentor would have shown me
how to make my life blaze with meaning
and by the time I had led the frowzy colleague away
along a hall and upstairs into oblivion and hurried back
my brilliant mentor was rather sternly speaking about Wordsworth
to some polite young people who showed due appreciation
away from which I skated sideways into a canvas garage
from which soon I drove a rickety blue truck on a mistaken road
but then checked a huge glowing map into which my boots descended
through a driftingly unsortable salad of signals all before dawn

and so reached a playground where my yellow-haired son played soccer
by kicking a big orange which grew more mushy as the game went on
which seemed necessary though not easy to explain on the phone
to my ex-wife who implied it was a bad time for soccer with an orange
since as she pointed out I had regrettably ignored
a responsibility to Aunt Margaret involving lemons
to which I replied "There was no parking on South Street"
after which long flights of concrete stairs led to a room of talkers
who knew all about Mexico where soon I was having to justify
all still before dawn in a letter to my lavish dark-haired former student
why I had followed her from office to office in a crowded suite
and kept reaching to touch her tanned hips—before dawn—

so that only a blasting hot shower and coffee could recover me
from the exhausting travail of being alive all night.

WHEELING

After Jane left, my plan was to write
either a novel called *Last Ditch*
or a nonfiction book called *Solitude of the Soul*.
I felt I should do this in a place
not already saturated with sadness and meaning;
I drove for half a day and stopped in Wheeling.

The hours were long in Wheeling.
I sat with my notebook beside Schenk Lake—
an old man drinking Dr. Pepper told me secrets about Obama.
In the lobby of the McLure Hotel a young woman asked me
what I was writing and smiled gently when I tried to explain.
Our relationship lasted almost twenty minutes—possibly
the high point of my Wheeling days. She had blonde hair
with a black stripe. Rhonda. Married to a cook at the hotel.

There was a neighborhood missing from Wheeling—it would be
more crowded, more intense, not so flat-out-plain in the sunshine,
there would be a rangy woman from some dark West Virginia valley
and she would appreciate the way I smiled right through
the solitude of our souls
and she would—something—it wouldn't *necessarily* be about sex.
She wasn't there.

At the East Wheeling Street Fair past Byron Street I ate fried pickles
and a band played music the equivalent of fried pickles
and for a few minutes I thought
I was getting close to the weird *other* Wheeling.

A palm reader with a crow tattooed on her arm informed me
that my palm predicted five years of being lost.
I said "I'll drink to that"
and drank a bottle of River City Ale and tried to chat
with a freckly woman whose auburn hair and sly jokey manner
led me not to anticipate her boyfriend in his Cleveland Indians cap,
a man made out of two hundred hamburgers.
For some reason he thought I was a critic reviewing the band
and he wanted to discuss the Red Hot Chili Peppers.
It was clear I gave him nothing to worry about
and the freckly woman just wanted to sell homemade jewelry.

That night I stayed forever at the Bridge Tavern
and made up my mind to join in football conversation
with some guys, to prove that being *in the world*
was really not difficult. After three beers I said "Hey,
that Bart Elby, he is one hell of a defensive halfback"
and I think a couple of the guys nodded vaguely
and I made further remarks in praise of Bart Elby
before one guy said firmly that there was no player for WVU
named Bart Elby and I said "Oh I meant the Charleston Threshers"
and soon they shifted away along the bar
and my empty glass held a chapter about solitude of soul.

Next morning I stood at one end of the Fort Henry Bridge
holding a sign HONK FOR THE SOLITARY SOUL—
three out of fifty cars honked—I dropped the sign in a waste bin—
weeds and glass fragments and plastic grocery bags
behind TJ's Sportsgarden held me still for long minutes—
I was having a deep Wheeling vision but it felt thin.

On my last Wheeling night I saw Rhonda in the lobby watching TV—
the Pirates losing to the Mets. "How's the writing?" she said.
"Maybe I should try Honolulu," I said. Rhonda said
"Whatever works!" I repeated her phrase several times
and she said I reminded her of Jack Nicholson
and she disappeared into the hotel kitchen.
I left Wheeling soon thereafter and drove home planning
a book called maybe *Lost But Not Dead* or *Whatever Works*.

PATHOS OF THE DETECTIVE

He drives his black Packard to the bar on Central Avenue.
Will the blonde show up? She has a way of moving
like a shadow dancing with itself. He feels

that this driving to Central Avenue and parking the Packard
with the blonde moving silently in his head
from a balcony across a lamplit mezzanine
is actually not a mere interim but the keynote of his life,
the low chord struck over and over
through any and all dazzling jeweled interruptions

so it's all pretty much a pipe dream, mug's game,
an endless Woolworth's for losers—

but you don't therefore lie down on the dumb pavement
or sink into a cat-haired sofa listening all day to the Dodgers
because there is at least the thin metallic dignity of
not simply doing that

so he tugs his fedora more firmly down on his brow
and he strides into the bar with his eyes going left and right
as if something a little too interesting might suddenly
step toward him on high heels and give the story a true jolt.

THRESHED OUT

Big pile of dirt near the Detroit airport
Magazines to the ceiling of the laundry room
Sprightliness for the Andrews Sisters was hard work

Idiosyncratic noises from anxious larynxes
Sing it now the silence is at the door
You want a cookie before it crumbles

She wants to be his cookie he wants to be hers
You will not be famous and powerful
Your dossier has slipped off the screen

Egg salad smothers your comic libretto
Big pile of dirt near the Detroit airport
Oh but let me touch the cookie

Authors writhe in unguent of wish
Sunshine hammering the glinty autos
I will not be famous and powerful

The message is everywhere the sorting is all hours
That certain someone has forgotten you
Glossies go in that bin over there

Many types of chaff
Imperturbable thresher

TOSSED

Well I'm a-gonna raise a fuss, I'm a-gonna raise a holler
'bout a world that crumbles and dumps everything including
old sailors in San Francisco and the passion of Gustav Mahler

———

Rain spashdashes against the window and trickles down into the mud
yeah kind of like our ambitions

———

Three years since Jim died—can that be true? Three years?

———

Everyone expendable, with bits to be recycled;
Spanish guitar gently implying this

———

There goes a woman on a bicycle, wearing black socks.
Her parents love her. To them she is not just any bicyclist
pedaling along in gray air with that unthrilling tattoo above her ankle.

———

You and me we are being thrown away.
In what may seem like slow-motion: being tossed

———

I hear the trash truck coming
metaphor sometimes is not our friend

———

Did you hear the news about Jack?
About Rachel? About Paul?

———

Quite a shock. It's quite—it's hard to believe.
Hard to take in. I'm still reeling

———

Another sweep of rain across the town square,
across the avenue, flakspacking the windows of the diner,
your hash browns are not warm anymore.

———

Yogurt is good. Thoughtful people eat yogurt.
But it comes in containers that are #5 plastic.
And your point is? If I drive three miles
to the Recycling Center I can recycle #1 and #2 plastic
but not #5. And your point is? There is a deep contradiction
in our system. There is a vast bland stupidity.
And your point?

———

So we've got this warehouse jammed with junked computers.
(On one of them your friend's friend wrote that novel
that almost won the I-Forget-Which Prize.)
We do some scavenging till it's not cost-effective,
then for the dangerous crap we lease a barge
and offload it at certain harbors in West Africa.

———

Big tray of spicy crabcakes. The caterers planned for a hundred people
but only sixty showed up. Can't we donate the crabcakes
to—some church or something? Dubious.
They've been on that table for three hours.

———

That sexy story you wrote when you were twenty-four—
your roommate said it was *hot*—
That reminiscence about your mother cheering nostalgically
for the Toronto Maple Leafs—
your uncle's friend said it was sweet

———

The editors thank you for your submission.
Despite whatever merits it may have
it doesn't quite match—it doesn't quite fit—

———

Spanish guitar in the next room or in your head

———

May seem like slow-motion

———

Can we recycle this? I doubt it.
We could put it in a box in the garage just in case.
That's crazy we can hardly walk in the garage already.
But look at this, you want this to end up in the ocean?
We didn't make the damn thing. Yeah but we bought it.
Come on come on just chuck it.

———

Spashdashing and trickling and puddling
and evaporating
can I give you a copy of my new chapbook
well I mean it was new just two years ago
would you like to have it would you keep it
I mean you wouldn't just toss it would you

———

gaspillage
un monde de gaspillage

———

Well, I just sent thirty dollars to the Basel Action Network.
The what? Basel Action Network. Google it.
Or are you too busy?

———

Mutability yeah old theme but this
exponential expirational exacerbation

Mutability yeah classic
but this ex ex ex

———

puddling
my new chapbook
he's a nice chap
composted
will you just toss it

———

Jim cared about people
not being trash. Three years already since he died?
Not to forget him.

ASSISTED LIVING

Just before the end there is a cake suffocated in sugar.
Its middle layer is banana cream.
On the long screened porch there is time and
time and time and time.
Someone says "Happy birthday to me"
hypnotized by the space where meaning was to have been.
The heat is not so good.
The ankles are not so good.
The towels, the sheets? Not too bad.
Mrs. Kaschisko in the next chair spits.
A ripple of adjustment crosses the porch.
When the young ones slip out
for a beer at the Swan Inn behind the dogwoods
you will have no idea.

———

. . . True enough—though
someone who looked at the right rare moment still
might see a baffled trace of imagination fugitive
like a fleet gibbon scrambling to find
in the chittering forest safer darker trees.

LIVIN' IN THE WORLD

I'm livin' in the world.
I said I'm livin' in the world.
My shirt is sweaty from the filmy hot sun
and I'm livin' in that. Yeah I'm livin' inside of that.

I got my old black shoes. You know the leather has creases.
I got my pale old face with some freckles, mmm-hmmm
you know it's got some creases. Baby I am so creased—
due to livin' in the world.

You think I'm not a big deal. Yeah well that's your point of view.
And you're livin' in that.
Oh I'm sure you've got your own troubles;
cuz baby look where you live:
I mean you're livin' in the world—
or so I have to assume! I mean I should be assumin'
that you are very human

but like, that's not my focus.
I said that's not what is my focus.
My head is full of my livin', sweaty heap of old livin'
in the self shop, mmm-hmmm,
I work long hours in the self shop.
Seem like I have to be a self;
job can't be done for me by nobody elf.

I'm walkin' Forty-Third and Locust.
You know my laundry's not done.
You know my novel's not done.

It's called *Livin' in the World*.
Every chapter is a cesspool!
And I'm a purple submarine.
You think you know what I mean.
But you don't care all that much.
You've got your spouse and house and such. . . .
All right, go think about them, if they give you a focus
but I'm back over here, in the heat on Forty-Third,
in the motion of the ocean down below each every word
because of livin' in the world.

You know my car engine sounds bad. It kind of smells like burnt toast.
Was made in 1985. It wants to give up the ghost.
But at least I have a car; I can drive into town.
Maybe stop at the bakery—get me some sourdough bread.
So then I come out of the bake shop,
I've got a parking ticket. Caused by livin' in the world.

I said I'm livin' in the world.
It's just an all-day buzz.
It is that in which I focus,
walkin' Forty-Third and Locust.

Well, you can take away my job.
You can say I have a shallow grasp of postmodern pluralism.
You can say I fail to excavate
the privilege encoded in the speech of my class.
In the speech of my social class, mmm-hmmm.
Yeah I have this privilege: it doesn't always feel so great,
it's like a shirt that's slightly itchy
but it fits into your theory—
that's how you might live in the world, by having a theory.
So then you have to live with that.

Oh the sun is blurry hot on Locust Street
and I am inside my sweaty shirt.
My narrow hungry life is buzzin' and I'm livin' in that.
You know, I've done some stupid things—I could give you a list.
I've done some chickenshit things,
yeah the list could get long.
But I am not dead in the world:

in my sweaty old Kansas City Royals shirt.
Yeah my Kansas City Royals shirt!
I don't see my other choice—
I keep on livin' in the world.

LINGO BISTRO

Night washes down across the land of subtle shrimp fondue
where three thinkers in bow ties are murmuring "angel of loss"
as the river opens its shimmering arms to the bosky vale
and the summer trees release their shadows into the soil.

High on the terrace above the latticed arbor of muscatel
one thinker bends his trimmest beard over a lavender dish
and glides by slightest motions of sensitive eyebrows
into the pond of nuance where evening grows sibilant

and another meditation on autumn will result, with cream.
The zephyr of filigreed perception blows so gently
you hardly might say "It blows" for fear of ruffling
the hairs above the thinker's terraced concentration.

Sibilant and sylphy and suggestive of a sarabande is
the language that arises, will arise, must surely soon
arise from far within the thinkers with their feelers
on the terrace above the latticed arbor of pinot noir,

the language, the lang the lang the lang there is so much
sheer language in the delicacy of the nuance in its pond
amid the words, which rhyme with birds, so much
implicit like lard in a fine pastry shell, so much

your tongue can only water! You can almost smell
the lavender water of the pool of night as you think
of Chinese chocolate and umbrellas as you feel
the feeling of the autumn trees as they whisper

in the dark, where the song of the oriole lingers
in the dark, while the spoons upon their saucers clink
on the terrace above the latticed arbor of pinot grigio
and out along the cooling boulevards in the dark

each feeler in his European chemise is murmuring
shadow of time, ribbon of mist, river of whispers,
lemon spumoni. Language. Through lozenges of light
you float away from me as if my bow tie were only memory

dappling the damask of evening above the bistros,
beyond the bosky vale in a shady Europe of the mind
as the darkening clouds do their wistful waltz
like an image of something something falling

with closed eyes as a feather falls
down to a white horse that canters into darkness
o'er trellised white roads to where the river's arms
hold out to silence her promising smooth first book.

NEW NEW POETICS

Glisten in wheeling light
of what's not your old stuff stuff the stuff
you already wrote fifteen articles about,
start up: wake: get
new—I'm new what's with you? Blaze
in the high-tech nano corridors of new thinking newer
than what you did dud did dudly think
begin—start—incipience as in
forerunning of the forewave of the indeterminate not-quite-yet of
spume of pre-forthcome experientiality as inhalation
auto-created in the modality of pelvic shove
as in Gertrude

Stein a continual present—my phrases one's phrases our phrases
endlessly cascadacious in non-co-opted self-unpacking fresh-packs
of primacy of liquidity of outreach vectored by re-de-dis-recognition of
"time" being culturally determined culturally mapped all clock-scummed by
culture whereby they, the they, they who do that oldy moldy poetics
in their old logo-pogo are all reified in smog of bad oldness
oh wake up you dead formalist hogs! *Begin* all hyperlinky good-fresh
as in Gertrude

Stein each thing within its own act of being each thing acting *into*
re-freed activation of its own not-yet-identity, of that, of through that
and inside behind that for and from its moment amongst cascade of moments
glistening (and *you* don't know how to write the articles about it but I do)
saturated with the am-ing of *am new* far in through behind what is to find
and simultaneously be found as originary, originative, not what got sold last week

not smelly stained sheets of old bad pseudo-transparent hegemonica no no
but dripping pulsing *echt* of Now This Oh Hey Now This thisly
telescoping its Chex Mix of implications in more than three ways
are you kidding more than *five* ways as in Gertrude

Stein may I have a drink of water please and as morph-limned above thus
refreshing our lang—oh do lang do lang
enacting the very act!—*begin* you fool give me your lips now
oh "god" vibratory with an acute hunger endlessly self-reflexive in the unquittable
asking of what does it mean? It means itself! Yes! Oh please do it faster
and after all wake *up* what do the leaves mean? They are the mean-*ing*
of themselves Christ it's all so gerundial—but you don't get it
no because it's New Now in a volcanic openness, openation in
the immediacy of the tactile, the never-never-yet-capitalized steaming viscous
residue bursted free from dialectical webs (please now) (we could have a margarita)
without autocratic prejudicial intervention of your old old yadda yadda so forth
can I touch your hip we must drain off the interpretive we need GENERATIVE
dislodging and downchucking old bad commodification *I'm new*
so what is with you? I mean right now as in Gertrude

Stein give me tenure now. I am ready. We generate, we begin!
Not old bad you see?
Glistening, now, into the breeze!

THANKS FOR YOUR BOOK

Thanks for your new book, the cover is nice,
quite striking really, and the title is kind of catchy
and I will read it when I get a chance—
well, I mean I'll read *in* it—
the days of "reading every page" seem so ancient now

but anyway yeah thanks for the book, and congratulations
of course, but I assume you have some perspective
on what isn't happening? I mean you do realize
how the world changed around 1989, right?
Up until 1989 there was still at least the dream
of "contribution to the great discussion"
and the Individual Talent revising the entire Tradition
and all that sweet marshmallow belief but then

in 1989 approximately that whole dream fractured
in a thousand directions like an Empire State Building
(oh funny quaint name) made of ice
being whacked on a hot city day whacked over and over
by the innumerable sledgehammers of LICSE
(Late Imperial-Capitalist Self-Expression) each sledge wielded
by a bright-eyed enfranchised citizen-dreamer hallucinating
that he or she was bolting a new steel block into the soaring edifice
which instead was getting riddled with innumerable busy cracks

WHACK WHACK every day since 1989 the shards of melting ice
cascade across the avenues glittery and shrinking
in the blaze of cacophonous plurality WHACK

and the sledging dreamers stagger puzzled and quivery
amid the deepening slushgushing unreadable rivulets that find
a thousand paths to the great sewer called How We Felt

which I mention just to make sure you have a clear perspective
and in that context, hey, thanks so much for your book.

GLANCERS

I saw you across the courtyard—you glanced my way;
then we were swept into the economy of needs and forces.

Like back in high school—high school goes on:
veneer vs. veneer; occasionally an effort to be truly present
but then swept—
among the poseur flocks. . . .

But some weeks after our glance
we did, one afternoon, talk
in the Common Room—for twenty minutes;
while others rustled the *Herald Tribune.*

Years later what lived in memory striped by shadows
thrown by columns of that courtyard
across the wood planks of the Common Room was sure to be
the wistfulness of glancing across a space—

which after all is why we made art:

my piece was a room of blue air empty except for
two blue chairs side by side, each chair made of blue rags
tied with blue string;

your piece was a sculpture of two hands
made of a thousand pencil erasers—
two hands nearly touching fingertips.

We won awards; and after the ceremony smiled glancingly at each other
in a moment better (briefly) than our works.

TALENTED YOUTH

All these talented persons under thirty-five can go
fuck themselves. Just kidding, they're fine,
so human and vivacious with their little tattoos
which are slightly pathetic as self-enhancements but hey
youth has to declare itself and the important thing is

they really have talent—not all of them but quite a few
and they stay up late at night blogging their heads off
not stupidly, or at least with quick bursts of intelligence
and some of them reveal that they actually do care
as opposed to just flourishing buzz moves like pom-poms

so I guess my role pretty much should be to stand aside
I mean I've got three times their income by now
and I've felt the Vitamin F rush of what felt
in a dozen weirdly brief spotlit venues like renown
so I should adjust to being a white-haired also-ran

whose crinkly gentle smile says "I agree I'm not great
but it was grand to aspire back in the day but now
the field is yours, give it your best shot even if it is
one hell of a longer shot than you can realize"
and not be a deluded old dude still grimly campaigning

for the lost cause of the deathless attractiveness I saw in my secret mirror
back when I too felt fizz-brash enough to say

Baboons of El Paso, cheerleaders of Pensacola,
tangerines flying through the soul of Des Moines,
desire is the torch in the cavern of the flimflam of time
and Savannah's guacamole will suffice in the orgy of tropes.

MILDEWED ANTHOLOGIES

Fragged and pre-emptingly disnerved am I
by megrims forthrising from the down-sucked
gravity-humbled fungal-damp discompositional
demotion/dismissal of disremembered claimants.
Their non-negotiable odor-sad weary-trope defunctness
sticks in my aspirational craw.

READER DEPRESSED

Basement full of books garage full of books—
and we leave our litter. . . .

Little glut-thicket of half signals and flicker-links within my skull
not efficiently organized for implementation of any 75-year plan

Faulty equipment tends to cause a mess

Oh not to leave my son and daughter with the depresso-heavy chaos
of nearly three thousand books

Those books will be archaic artifacts in the electro-digitized world
of my old age—coming along in years like days—

nearly three thousand archaic artifacts: depressing
simply for being of a disappearing life; also
most of them depressing because I never did read them
because I was so much smaller than my fantasies
and a person is terribly finite; but also
maybe nine hundred of them depressing in another way
because I did read them or read in them and marked them
with my finicky marginal notes tending to make those books unbearable
for any conceivable next reader;
we use and we use and we leave our litter.

When I turned fifty I think I passed a point not realizing it
I passed beyond the phase of my life in which I could believe
each book I read would contribute to the great

assemblage of understanding, the great coherence
to be built in my spirit—

spirit which turns out to be too entangled in
the little glut-thicket of disorganized flicker-links. . . .

My father when he was eighty-six said quietly
that he didn't expect ever to read *The Brothers Karamazov*
and his eyes looked far past the walls of his room.

HIS ALLEY METAPHOR

He wanted a figure for how his disease (which would kill him within a year)
seemed—he said it was as if

he'd been walking briskly along a busy sunny street
full of bananas and scooters and actors and sex
on his way to a lunch date with someone of quirky allure
when for no special reason he turned aside into an alley,
not even an alley but a shady ignominious passageway
that promptly grew more narrow and darker and then
still only a few feet from the bright fluttering street
he found that his life was now this grimy dark passageway
which was not a passageway to anything visible
as it seemed to end in dark concrete a little farther along
and though he could still hear the honking and clacking
of people on their way to multiple stimulations
his eyes filled with the nothing but stained and forgotten concrete

and I thought this was a good metaphor
more obvious than some metaphors but with justification
and I hoped my friend might get a little satisfaction
maybe from writing down his metaphor and maybe publishing it
though he seemed less "ambitious" than in recent years
and more interested simply in finding that a friend of his
could for a minute really get what he meant.

THE ONE FOR HER

The one she's looking for—I can't seem to write it.
There would be a relevance—the color of a real day;
the weariness and the necessary persistence—

across the street a Michelob truck is backing up
in front of the Touchdown Tavern; two clerks on a break
are smoking behind Dolphin Seafood; from a rusty dumpster
a broken rocking chair protrudes; the streets vibrate
with ignorance of what ultimately to do;

she crosses at the light and passes the Verizon Wireless store
sensing absence of the one, the true—which I don't write—

instead I keep rephrasing my normal anxieties
as if they were unusual, as if it were rather witty of me
to feel them. This gives her a quiet twinge of disappointment
so familiar that it can barely be disappointing

and she turns the page, already forgiving me
as you would a child who can't stop building towers
that noisily collapse. . . . She even picks out a phrase to praise
while her spirit turns aside watching for some shadow of

the one for her. It would know the unsexy uncynical effort
of going on: it would know the dry patience of a waitress;
the air of a parking lot grime-dark with rain;
the look in a thin man's eyes when he said "one more chance";
the sadness hooked into a song called "Rough and Rocky"
and the fending off of sadness by someone putting on sneakers
at 5:15—there would be such a relevance—so she keeps looking.